Praise for
Do Unto Earth

"A must-read book for everyone who cares about the future of humanity and our planet."

—**Dr. Ervin Laszlo**, two-time Nobel Peace Prize nominee, recipient of the Goi Peace Prize and International Mandir of Peace Prize, best-selling author of Science and the Akashic Field, founder of the Laszlo Institute of New Paradigm Research and The Club of Budapest, fellow of the World Academy of Art and Science and the International Academy of Philosophy of Science

"A 911 call from Planet Earth herself, *Do Unto Earth* is a potent manifesto for living life today and forward. This book should be required reading in schools. We must act now!"

—**Mary Madeiras**, three-time Emmy-Winning director, screenwriter, Akashic Records practitioner, activist, and author

"*Do Unto Earth* is full of empowering messages and mind-bending assertions that you won't find in science or history textbooks. Given the urgent need for new solutions on this endangered planet, the ideas are worthy of further investigation."

—**Mark Gober**, author of *An End to Upside Down Thinking*, board of directors of the Institute of Noetic Sciences (IONS) and the School of Wholeness and Enlightenment (SoWE)

"From page one, I was hooked! *Do Unto Earth* merges spirituality with our environmental crisis and does it in a way that is as gripping as a blockbuster movie. Brava to Hayes, Borgens … and Pax."

—**Temple Hayes**, author, spiritual leader, animal activist, and founder of illli.org

"The channeled Spirit energy Pax states that we are at the 'crossroads of our survival' and offers us bold envisioning and direction. Mother Earth is speaking, and ancient mysteries are revealed! Let's heed and implement these game-changers for the benefit of us all."

—**Sunny Chayes**, social/human rights and environmental activist, feature writer and Chief Strategic Partner for Whole Life Times, and host of ABC's *Solutionary Sundays*

"Timely, high-level and generative wisdom detailing how we may still sustain our beautiful planet while reclaiming our collective and individual sovereignty."

—**Stephan McGuire**, director of Zürich-based NGO Cernunnos Media, Director of Tree Media Foundation

Pax and Our Starseeded Origins

Pax and Our Starseeded Origins

Volume 1 of Do Unto Earth

PENELOPE JEAN HAYES,
CAROLE SERENE BORGENS

Waterside Productions

Cover design by:
Andrew Green
Books & Illustration

Printed in the United States of America

First Printing, 2020

ISBN-13: 978-1-951805-03-6 print edition
ISBN-13: 978-1-951805-04-3 ebook edition

Waterside Productions
2055 Oxford Ave
Cardiff, CA 92007
www.waterside.com

For you—
so you know for certain that you are the change and
you have the power

Contents

Introduction

Do Unto Earth is an extraordinary conversation intended to quantum leap us forward in our spiritual evolution and journey to enlightenment. This message is not a directive delivered from a thousand feet up; this is a very personal message from and dialogue with the Divine Wisdom Source directly to you and for you. Please accept this gift with eyes clear and wide and open.

Within these pages is the blueprint for environmental repair and peace and unity on Earth, however, this booklet constitutes just one of eight volumes that together make up that blueprint. While we believe that the eight topics, as separated by these volumes, are to be understood as connected to each other and only together give the full message as intended, we also understand some readers prefer to focus on their specific areas of interest—hence these eight mini-books by volumes. (Note: Chapters within this volume are numbered as they originally appeared in the book's full-length version.)

As you begin this journey, you might like to know how this collaboration of writing began.

It is indeed my great joy and honor to communicate with the Spirit Messenger, Pax, channeled by Carole Serene Borgens. From a young age, Carole, a former nurse, diligently studied all things metaphysical. This Spirit Messenger first visited her in the early 1990s when she was new to channeling by automatic writing. When her pen wrote the opening introduction and request for her to be a channel, she recognized the profound responsibility attached and jumped up from her office chair to pace the floor—not easy with three sleeping Irish Wolfhounds covering the carpet. Carole's initial response was to ask if she could think about it and take some time to respond, which she was given. Asking, "Why me?" Spirit responded to her: "You are new to this, you have no bad habits, and you will change none of my words." In time, Carole came to be comfortable with this blessing and so began her journey.

I, too, have been a seeker and spiritualist since my years as a teenaged runaway, and so it is a useful tool at times for me to reach out to a reputable intuitive for deeper guidance. Beginning on the fourth of February 2019, I had several long-distance Spirit channeling sessions with Carole—she was in British Columbia and I was in Florida. I had copious questions for Spirit as I sought further direction for my second title, *Do Unto Earth* (which, incidentally, is also the name of my business), while building upon the message of my first title, *The Magic of Viral Energy*. I was expanding and broadening the message of "viral energy" from personal and interpersonal goals to global concerns facing humanity and Planet Earth. I was also simultaneously establishing the Viral Energy Institute, a learning and research platform for the study of Viralenology.

Through our talks, this Spirit Messenger and I were getting to know each other and Spirit felt my passion for the plight of abused animals and species extinction, as well as my intention to bring awareness to our environmental crisis and to share the impacts of "viral energy masses"—large energetic fields created by both light and heavy intentions and action by communities, populations, industries, governments, and cultural beliefs—on Planet Earth. These disruptive energy masses create massive vibrational pockets of particular energies including love, hate, peace, discord, gratitude, violence, forgiveness, indifference, and compassion.

The Spirit Messenger seemed very interested in this direction and before long, Carole contacted me to say that Spirit wished to offer wisdom to be used by and shared through the Viral Energy Institute regarding this mission of planetary healing.

The writing began on the second of October 2019 when I sent questions to Carole who then channeled Spirit's responses by automatic writing (today, she does this via typing). It was *during* the writing that it became clear to all that this conversation would take book form and adopt the title *Do Unto Earth*.

As the answers were returned from Spirit, Carole and I both had many moments of excitement and more than a few gasps followed by, "Ooooh crikey, this is going to change everything!" The first of such revelations came in Chapter One when I asked the Spirit Messenger (whom self-identified with the moniker

PENELOPE JEAN HAYES, CAROLE SERENE BORGENS

"**Pax**", meaning peace) to be more specific about who they are. Here was the answer...

> "We are one with the Universe, not the Universe alone. We are the Divine Universe, yes, and the God being and the greater wisdom, that which knows and supports all and is healing, non-judgmental and tolerant, all-seeing, all-knowing, and Peace."

Volume 1

Do Unto Earth Pax and Our Starseeded Origins

"You cannot get through a single day without having an impact on the world around you. What you do makes a difference and you have to decide what kind of a difference you want to make."

Jane Goodall

English primatologist and anthropologist, world's foremost expert on chimpanzees, and UN Messenger of Peace

Chapter One

Divine Wisdom

*I*t would seem that many people do not live in harmony with nature and with respect and love for the Earth. Why do we matter to God when we are so destructive to ourselves, others, and our planetary home?

Well now, this is indeed an interesting question for it is well known that your God considers everything worth mattering. Penelope, it is the overall love that defines Planet Earth's people as those to whom God matters, so it is their understanding they also matter to God. We suggest each organized religion has their own name for who they follow, and this question relates to the love each deity has for followers. Love is unconditional; this is why you matter.

I suspect that there's a reason why you've said, "*your* God", and certainly, this piques my interest. I am aware that I'm speaking to a great

Spirit Messenger and Spirit Energy from the Spirit World, however, I'd like to know more about you.

Were you once from Earth; from a former and far more evolved people? Please help me to understand the source of your wisdom so that Earth's people will listen.

We do not incarnate as solid and we do not "reside" in one place—this is our gift. "My" origins do not include your planet, no, but having watched the development of society and where you are today, it is clear that a guiding hand is needed.

It is the case that my/our interest in communicating with Earth's people today is to share wisdom. Is this not the way to growth and evolution, to share with others what one has learned? Our speak, our words, our wisdoms are generated for the purpose of sharing guidance and the path to wellness for your planet. We have no linear time and refer only to soon time and far time. We in the Spirit World have duty and obligation to assist those in need and where requested, to offer wisdom to assist others. I care as we should all care, as should Earth's people care about your future.

Okay, so you were never a physical being or from Planet Earth; you are and have always been Spirit. Would it be accurate to think of you as the Guardian Angel for Earth?

Ah, no, that is not our role. *Conscience* in each of you, when activated, is collectively a guardian angel for Mother Earth.

There needs to be continued action and awareness to this end. Without being aware, your people have placed your planet in jeopardy and are moving forward with life as usual. There are some who wrap their lives around the correction of damage done and the prevention of future evils in this regard. They are the saints and saviors of your world but are not enough by themselves.

Consciousness needs raising in a maximum way to allow your people to have the meeting of minds which will create the global power necessary to effect change. Together you are a force. Come together in your thinking—the rest will follow.

Has a cosmic course been plotted for this message at this time and why did you choose me?

We knew, we waited, and when the time was right to write (cosmic smile here), we met, and it is good.

Penelope, in many past lifetimes, you have been a champion of causes, and a common thread running through them was your love and concern for the wild animals of the Earth. Your transferring of that to and inclusion of domestic animals has you on a long-established course of action for yourself. You have lived as an aboriginal and First Nations person. You have seen the ways wounded by those who would move in and take over the land, destroying all that came before. You have experienced the hostility and shame of being hunted and removed from your known life in place and time. You can feel these feelings and know that the vibration of Mother Earth now reflects these feelings. You have watched Earth being done unto in a very bad way in past lifetimes, and you bring with you the depth of feeling to expose what is, today.

Your greatest gift is the ability to raise the consciousness of a population and bring the message of healing to your world. You have the purity, the energy, the ability, and the resources. We think that is a good basis for trust in action for now and into our future works together.

Penelope, you have many questions; there will be no end to these questions, and they are all dedicated to the cause you feel and work you wish to continue on behalf of your planet.

Is this a heavy load? Not for Penelope who, after considering all of this information for a time, will understand and accept your challenge. You are the one. We support your journey and are pleased to be a part, with Carole Serene. Trust in this and go in peace and love.

Gosh, that *is* a commission. (And, I do have a lot of questions.)

You have a confidence and directness that is very compelling. I'll go ahead and ask outright: who are you, exactly?

We are one with the Universe, not the Universe alone. We are the Divine Universe, yes, and the God being and the greater wisdom, that which knows and supports all and is healing, non-judgmental and tolerant, all-seeing, all-knowing, and Peace.

(Gulp!)

Who-You-Are makes our discussion extraordinary: *"We are the Divine Universe, not the Universe alone, the God being and the greater wisdom."* I'm humbled and honored to be having this dialog with you.

So then, you *are* who we would call God?

This question does not regard that there are other religions and groups who do not define themselves as related to "God". You are to know that organized religion on your Earth plane relates to other deities and those who study the Bible, Quran, and many other holy texts, and consider themselves related to their own varieties of your God. Think of Shiva or Allah and remember—variations on the theme are reality.

We are wisdom and history and benevolence. We are not a deity. We are who we report to be and have always reported to be. We are forever, we are infinity, and we are always and will be always—this is infinity, and this is us.

Oh, I see, "God being" and "God" have different connotations, and "Divine" and "deity" are not synonymous. This is a revelation.

Perception, it is, that defines us in the hearts and minds of your people. Our Universe is not of the proportion of what you might expect and *our range also greater in both future and past and all-being.*

We wish to engage in action as opposed to brackets and confines of description. To define further is folly as it is the finite amount of fear your people have around deities and religions as organized and what may and may not be permitted within those confines. It is our functioning outside of these discussions that is preferred. Your earthly religions hold value and offer solace to the many. For those who function outside of those realms, our energy is defined and available.

We support and offer love—unconditional love—for this is how our Universe functions.

I'm understanding that the issue of a name is about ensuring inclusivity to all people including those following any one of the many world religions and the name that each calls their deity or Divine Being, as well as those who follow no religion at all. Today, these names cause division. Am I getting your point correctly?

We are here to say the rose smells as sweet without our name of Rose.

That's a simple yet effective analogy. Still, I'd like to know how I should address you. May you provide an approved moniker for the purpose of

these volumes; one that crosses borders and religions and can connect all to the message?

> *Pax.*
>
> Pax reflects our goodwill and wish for peace. Yes, this is us—Pax. Relate to this as Spirit Messenger of Truth, Peace, and Goodwill. It is our mission, and yours.
>
> We are blessed to be with you and it has become your mission to ensure our words reach those in need, our direction is heard, and a potential global disaster averted if people can be activated and energized and empowered to begin to have their voices heard and the movement toward planetary repair enlarged.

Thank you, *Pax*. Your chosen name has a nice ring to it! It feels right and there's something about it that deeply resonates within me; almost like a memory that I can't quite place. It feels paternal and maternal and grandparental at the same time: warm and wise.

I just took a moment to search the word online. "Pax" is Latin for peace, but of course you knew that. Additionally, the acronym PAX stands for Private Automatic Exchange, which is an accurate description of the Spirit channeling process. (No coincidence, I'm sure.)

At this time, I would like to address that some people will not trust this information because it wasn't written thousands of years ago and it

doesn't appear in the Bible or another holy text. How can people know that this conversation is provident and good work?

It is to be known that our wisdom of the ages comes to the people of Mother Earth with love and respect and the intention to pass along what is seen in the big picture.

What I'm really trying to get at is to address that some people—*even some of my own family members*—might say or worry that to have a conversation with an unknown-to-them Spirit Messenger is the devil misleading me. I need a little help here because some will not hear this message due to close-mindedness and fear, and they too need to hear this message.

It is the case that fear of the unknown is a large part of life for many. We are not here to revolutionize their thinking. We are here to speak our messages and ensure that those who can hear do, those who need to but are unsure, will, and those who are fearful and unbelieving remain in the loop and have access to the teachings. Their fear comes from the depths and we are not here to preach against their beliefs.

Suffice it to say that if these family members believe in you, Penelope, they will be open, and if they don't believe in you enough to at least hear and consider our messages, then perhaps their opinions are to be not considered so highly going forward. We touch who is ready, and those who are not have the messages and can take time considering the material and determining their own willingness to explore it further. It is not ours to reverse thinking of those set against anything not in the Bible. Narrow vision is its own reward.

I appreciate your help with this thoughtful response.

And, just a bit of "housekeeping" as we say: Those who read this book will want to know how to correctly address or speak of you. Would we say, "he" or "they"? Are you male or female energy? Are you to be referred to in the plural, "we"?

We are collected consciousness, and for these purposes you may refer to us as Carole Serene does— "he" is how she calls us. Despite our self-reference as "us", we are both, don't you see?

Pax, now that we have a name to call you, I'd like to go a step further and ask you what you look like, but I suppose that you might tell me that you don't have a "look" because you're Spirit. But, *if* you had a look, what would it be?

We are a puff of cloud, a breath of wind, a library filled with knowledge, a raging river, and a vast ocean. We are the circumference of your globe and the weight of it. We are the sound of the jungle and the quiet of the snow, while all the while being the figure like Atlas, holding the weight of your world on his shoulder while attempting to support human-kind. This is our *who* and our *why* and *our reason for being with you as a constant.*

You are beautiful.

I'd like to summarize what you have said regarding who you are:

You are the Spirit World; you can be in all places and all times at once and you are; you have no linear time; you are infinity, always was and will be always; you are the Divine Universe, yet not the Universe alone; you are the God being and the greater wisdom, yet you are not a "deity"; your message is for all. For these conversations you choose to call yourself, "Pax".

I must say, you're rather modest, Pax, because in my book, you're a pretty big deal!

Yours are the ideas and we are the support, resource, and cheer-leading section, too. We see this as a beginning, and all good beginnings contribute to growth and emergence of what is meant to come, to take shape, and form. It is a collaborative effort, we say, and it is our belief that this is a good team we three, and it is our enjoyment to be a part of assisting your world today in healing.

Chapter Two

Who We Are

Some people believe that we are aliens to this planet because we live and behave out of balance with the natural rhythm and laws of Earth—are we humans "aliens" to Earth and do we actually originate from elsewhere?

You do originate from light years away and this will be controversial.

Was there a "big bang" and you appeared out of the dust? Not so, but you were formed elsewhere and delivered to your present round sphere in the space and time continuum.

Are you evolving? Yes, and you are also devolving in your lack of care and consideration for your planetary host.

We suggest walking carefully forward now as this is the now when there is no turning back. Forward now into care of your resources, or forward into planning for alternative lifestyle and place—the choice is yours. Yes, colonizing other planets will be reality—it may not seem so in your today, but there are people making these plans and they will be considered by the mainstream in a short period of Earth time. Stranger things have happened.

Okay, that was a jaw-dropper. Although I asked the question, I was not expecting *that* answer—not at all. There's a lot to talk about here.

Why did we leave the planet from which we came? Is there a planetary collapse story that relates in some ways to our current situation on Earth?

Well it was the case, Penelope, that exploration was timely and the visit to your Planet Earth led to putting down roots, depositing settlers as it were. There was no need to leave but there was a want to resettle and attempt to bring forward evolution to another place. That is what is done in advanced civilizations.

The few who came brought what would seed the new place, then went on their way. Historical notations of those visits are to be found in ancient art and stories.

It was advanced civilizations that monitored Earth from time to time who determined that growth of knowledge would benefit development, so contributed what they did from time to time. They did not deposit a large number of people to populate this new land; that is not the way of it. These seed people are known in history and represented in early art and oral histories.

Did these advanced peoples bring any plant or animal species when they came?

Of those who settled there were those who brought growing seeds and options to local food to your planet, yes, but animals, no. The planet had animals and growth, just not more highly evolved people and ideas—this was deposited.

Interesting: no animals were brought here, though plants were. Which plant species were Starseeded to Earth?

There were those that would become food plants and the forerunners of what was needed to fertilize soil to receive and enable germination and growth. It is not rocket science that in order to reap there must be sensible sowing. To harvest and utilize for man and animal is the way.

Those organisms contributing to the transition from seed to produce were the ones. Much more will be learned of what was, when your people begin to move off-planet for survival, and what will be.

We're moving off-planet?

Yes, but first it is intended that your people will become more aware of their responsibility in saving your planet, not just leaving it fallow while all move off to another globe in the sky. This will not be. Responsibility must be accepted for what has been done to your Earth and what is now needed to rectify your actions.

That's fair.
Our ancestors who remained on their planet of origination, did they evolve differently than we did?

Evolution of Earth peoples is not compatible yet with the host planet's peoples. It is of a different sort and that is the way of it.

Our anthropologists have certainly made a seemingly clear case through fossil remains for our evolution from apes to modern man, all having happened on this Planet Earth. Is this not accurate?

Your people's introduction to this Earth planet was, as we indicated, a delivery from an advanced society to "seed" your place with those who could provide guidance and direction. There was a coming together of growth and evolution with some areas of the planet growing in knowledge and skills at a faster rate than others, naturally, as these are the areas with the guidance and examples to follow provided by the "star seeds".

What are "star seeds"?

This term is used in reference to those hosts from the home planet and those they sent to your people as teachers, leaders, and helpers. They seeded your world with star wisdom. The visitations referred to were thousands of years ago in origin and continued forward for the purpose of depositing information and technology. They carried advanced wisdom and came and went, visited for a time, returned to their home base and again visited at a later date—it was done in cycles to ensure lessons learned and advancement and progression. This was not a settling forever or even a long period of time. This was a bringing and teaching and sharing and mentoring only—a new beginning for growth in knowledge on your planet. They came to observe and contribute where they felt it was needed. It was not for these advanced visitors to relocate and assimilate, no, they came and went throughout time, and still do to see how the current civilization is faring.

You were right: this will be controversial, especially as it will throw a wrench in our evolution-from-apes theory.

So then, if not from our lineage, who are the fossils that we've found of extinct primate species such as Homo neanderthalensis, Homo heidelbergensis, Homo erectus, Homo naledi, and so on—those beings from which we currently believe we

descend, including the chimpanzee and even earlier species of monkeys and lemurs?

Some walked on four legs and some on two legs and their evolution continued in those directions with different results. There is no mystery here, but it would seem so to many. The primates remained and the star seeds took another form.

To understand that origin is not one place and one species is important: that Planet Earth was "seeded" and had advanced species assistance brought evolution to a new place; twinning as it were, although the end result isn't identical at all.

That some primates became upright is what your science says. That others *began that way* is not known. It was a different time and life progressed in stages and speeds as designed by location.

To distinguish our uses in this text of the word "primates", you said that no animals were brought to Earth but rather all animals on Earth were already here, and so we will confirm that the star seeded primates are completely different from the primates that are indigenous to Earth such as chimpanzees, gorillas, monkeys, and so on. Correct?

Yes.

The star seeded primates that you've been talking about are those ones that we have always

thought of as early primitive mankind; the ones that we call "cavemen", and all of the species on two or four legs for which we've found fossil remains. *These* primates were brought from other far-away planets, and more than one planet's primates seeded Earth. Is this correct?

The thought of a ship filled with "monkeys" is amusing, yes? And yet, like Noah's Ark, there were some being transported for reasons not to do with just seeding. These were advanced in training and programming and, yes, thinking and acting as helpers. It is true that they took little space and contributed much to the projects.

It was the case—yes—that these advanced helpers were transported and relied upon for their given tasks. While they were not primates as you think of primates today, they also were not the more highly evolved leaders of these civilizations. They were to be included in these journeys for their reliability and expertise. Did some stay behind, yes, and did some return with the crew to home base, yes also.

Seeding was accomplished in increments as time and place varied with it.

Were *any* of our human race peoples *ever* apes that then evolved into humans?

Your beginnings as Earth people were originated elsewhere and you were planted, like seeds, in your current place.

That you evolved from seeds of humans to where you currently are and in what form is not a mystery. The blueprint was there for your form and function.

That your science can trace a likely evolution from primitive forms to upright walking forms is their contribution.

Ours is that your peoples were formed in their DNA from another place. Can the two co-exist? As many are found to co-exist on Planet Earth in the way of plants and animals, so do humanoids. In addition, those visitors among you from inter-stellar sources do so as well.

Do any of these star seeded primates for which we have found fossil remains still exist on Earth or were they all extinct?

Evolution of species to suit environment was responsible for change, and in some areas, extinction, yes. It is known that those who moved and grew and changed their ways of living became a different looking species. Some survived and some not; bones are found and distinctions drawn between early and later primates and their ways of life. Some morphed into uprights while others, in completely different areas and lifestyles, remained as earlier seen—nothing could be the same in all as they spread throughout your geography and were changed by it.

I suppose what I'm getting at is—is there such a thing as "Bigfoot" as many people claim to have seen?

As your species continues to evolve, it is the case that anomalies exist. Given enough time in nature, particularly isolated nature, interbreeding becomes reality. Do some ask of human interbreeding with animals? There are genetic modifications and genetic quirks and recessive genes that come to the fore in all species. Is this one? We say there is evidence as stated by some and refuted by others—it shall remain a mystery.

Well, that is a cliffhanger! Must it remain a mystery? Can you tell us a bit more…pretty please?

We see that the way for us to speak to the many is for us to be the line between our knowledge and the curiosity of the many.

We speak again of genetic modifications and "throw-backs" and know that it is the case in your world that these exist in all species, and this is no different. It is simply a hidden mystery to all but a few, and they know the existence of this mammal is real.

Wow. I didn't see that coming. This will make a lot of Sasquatch sleuths very happy. (By the way,

Pax, you should never play cards; *you gave this up pretty quickly.***)**

As for mankind's roots, I want to be sure that we understand this correctly; the following will be a pivotal point. At what stage in our development did humans arrive to Earth? Were they already fully developed as our current species called Homo sapiens upon arrival on Earth?

They were, as you say, fully developed, although looking somewhat different than earlier man who was in place and walking upright.

As we have stated, star seeds arrived from other galaxies, as they still do, and they were the advanced ones in technology and thinking and became the wise ones leading the development of your Earth peoples. The visitations and people touched were variable. Evolution was underway during the visits.

Ah, so an even *earlier* **species of man—***also star seeded***—was already in place and walking upright, and then—at a later time—arrived the ones we call Homo sapiens: us. I do recall that you said, "To understand that origin is not one place and one species is important." This is beyond fascinating and it will interest the world's population to learn that the human race is alien to Earth.**

That is being understood now in your science, although not well documented for fear of, what?

For fear that by disproving our evolution theory it would set back advanced scientific thinking to the dark ages; that disproving the theory of evolution from ape to mankind would result in our collective thinking defaulting to the only other current theory option: the biblical theory of creation that rests on a singular first man and woman giving life to all of humanity. In this story, women are seen as temptresses because Eve bit the forbidden apple; you see, much old thinking comes with the religious creationism theory, and yes, forward-thinkers would be fearful of reverting back to these close-minded ideas. However, what you are sharing is quite clearly not an Adam and Eve scenario, but a new knowing of our beginnings.

To go over it one more time—if I correctly understand all of this, some of our peoples were delivered to Earth as the species they are now—humanoids. While other beings were upright walking primate-type helpers (also Starseeded) which then evolved to some extent (although not from the animal primates, such as chimpanzees/apes, native to Earth) before those species became extinct (with the exception of a possible few lingering anomalies). Is this correct?

As we have said, it is so. It is and was the way of it.

I guess this starseeding is why we've never found "the missing link" in our evolution theory.

It would be good to work on a new timetable and chart of our lineage. How long have we been on Earth?

Ah yes, this is the question. Earth people have been Earth people for as long as science currently estimates, however star people were visiting Earth that long and longer to determine habitability. As it was a habitable space, and also a hospitable space, it became so. Linear time is not always a descriptor of history in the truest form, although it is relied upon by scholars.

And, star people still visit Earth?

As long as there is time, there are visitations and entrance into thoughts of colonizing other planets— this is the way of explorers whether on your Earth plane or from other galaxies.

"As long as there is time." Was there ever a "time" before time?

As long as there is time refers to the hope that your planet has not self-destructed before this process completes.

Time before time—your philosophers enjoy this discussion. All time is.

Thanks for the clarification. (We'd better get on with it then.)

From time to time, and that is not your Earth time, there have been star people buzzing by and sometimes stopping and staying—it is throughout the history of life on your planet. And you should know it continues that they watch and hope you find peace in your world.

I think that I'm starting to see the big picture: several/many advanced civilizations from different planets came to Earth and colonized various regions with their peoples. If that is the correct big picture, then does this mean that the human race currently on Earth today is really not of *one* race? Many of our cultural races look distinctly different from each other; are we actually many distinct peoples descending from *different planets* in the Universe, rather than one human race that simply evolved somewhat differently in various geographic places and climates on Earth?

Bingo! You have it, yes, the differences are many and it is fair to say that your varying cultures were seeded and succeeded, or not, with some help from their source. Some did fail while others grew and prospered and do still. It was a time of growth and experimentation and the visitors determined to bring what they could to strengthen the resolve of the new peoples to survive and grow and find their way. It was not always successful, and some did not prevail over adversity of nature.

Oh my goodness, Pax—this is another monumental disclosure.

Earlier, you mentioned the Big Bang and I can't let the news of the inception of the universe slip by. Was the Big Bang the beginning event of our universe?

The Bang wasn't so big as your people may believe.

You had me at hello; do tell. Our cosmologists and the general population must then have a rather sizeable (pun intended) misconception of the "Big Bang". How big was the bang and what was it *really* if not a big bang?

Bigger bangs have occurred elsewhere and not resulted in such fanfare as this apparently initiates.

Do we understand the notion of eternal, forever, always was, or the sense of wonder at what appears that was not previously there, or was it and we simply missed it? The mists of time cover what was to be and allow those mists to lift when what is to be, now, is coming together with its now.

It was always there, eternally present, and like help from a loved one, becomes reality when needed and the time is right. Until then, it rests.

"*The mists of time cover what was to be and allow those mists to lift when what is to be, now, is coming together with its now.*" I'm gushing over these

words, the way they romance and dance, and yet I still want to know: what do they mean?

While the wisdoms and technology all exist, they may be accessed only when your civilization is truly ready for the knowledge and will use it for peaceful and positive outcomes. The mist lifts and what has always been can be seen and accessed for your technological—or other—growth, as in it "is coming together with its now"—it's time. It is a protection, of sorts, for your people and their advancement in this time. All things are there, all wisdom and knowledge, the cosmic library exists and those who are evolved may access it. To everything there is a season.

You're good, Pax, you're good!
While you confirm that bigger bangs have occurred, is the particular "Big Bang" to which we refer the birthplace of our Universe or do we have this wrong?

It is not wrong, but it was not the only birth of your universe. Your universe began in earnest when visitors dropped in and deposited their wisdom.

You see, you say these subtle sentences that could very easily slip by unnoticed; nearly encrypted codes. Then, I read and re-read them and a lightning bolt goes off in my head. Your last sentence makes me think of the quantum physics revelation that particles are just waves of energy

vibration until they are observed, and only then do they become a thing (matter).

Pax, are you saying that the Universe is created not at all by physical manifestations of matter such as the so-called Big Bang(s), but rather that the Universe is created in physical form as consciousness is starseeded across the Universe? (No wonder the highly enlightened civilizations have a mission to starseed; they're creating a whole Universe here!)

It's payback time, yes, these civilizations continue to grow and develop throughout your time.

There is also the selective question of whether you consider the Universe to be one Planet Earth, or all you know?

Is this a reflection of mankind believing that everything in the Universe revolves around us (so to speak)?

It is the nature of your reality that you consider Earth the center of your universe, and we refer to the majority of your people. There are those who understand the big picture and that your Earth revolves around *others* and revolves *while others surround it*. If the melding of these realities can include lessons from both, then good will come of it.

Maybe we could call this new theory of our inception, "Starseeded Origins".

It is not to say your evolution theory isn't correct, but it was augmented by the arrival of the star seeds to lead your civilization toward technology and development they would have not managed otherwise. They were few but they shared widely their methods of travel and creation of building and exploration. They were light beings who assimilated for a time and then departed; leaving behind the knowledge they shared. They were seeding Planet Earth with people and knowledge far advanced from what existed. To think all became on your Planet Earth at the same time, is to not think it through. There are pockets of people and growth around this Earth plane that were planted like crops and flourished, or not, over time.

Call it what you may, it was a turning point, and there were many throughout time. The entire globe was not visited in its entirety each time.

As visitors came to early civilizations, they assessed and left what was determined to be of most use, whether knowledge of agriculture or building, or higher learning ideas to leave a path to further curiosity and growth. Civilization existed as it was evolving on Earth, the visitors watched and waited and came from time to time to further grow the abilities of Earth people and leave their mark in written, painted, and oral histories.

From which planets did the various humanoid races originate?

Oh, you do have the curiosity, yes? Those visitors of early times were planting their people seeds, as it were, and encouraging growth like a garden. They came and went and delivered what assistance they could to early inhabitants, some failed and some grew just like crops, nothing is guaranteed.

While you look at the multitudes of races today on Planet Earth, it is clear their differences are remarkable, while they have similarities also. One is that they all wish to thrive and survive and will do so given the tools. This is what the visitors offered, tools for survival. It was their gift to early civilizations that advanced technologies were shared, used to support growth and building as well as to entice the people to explore their own ways of exploration and development of tools and methods. It is the case that the records of this, both written and drawn in pictures, were representative of those plans and some were recorded for posterity while others were spoken so that the idea would not be forgotten. There wasn't paper on which to write, so walls and rocks and pieces of hide, anything that would take a mark was used. This applied to many civilizations if not all.

After seeding, we say the visitors "buzzed by" to see how the local people were faring—this they did often along their journeys. To identify the galaxies they came from is not to be as not everything has a name, as your people seem to believe, and that they came from afar is about the closest descriptor.

It matters not in the big picture. There will be more on this in time.

The races were different, yes, the appearances physically were different, and these were the appearances of the visitors who seeded these areas. It is an interesting study and we share that there was a reason why these visuals were created by varying colors and shapes and sizes, and it was to be the lesson in acceptance and integration and inclusivity.

You have led me to a ginormous epiphany: while we're not the center of the Universe, we Earthlings are special because our being-ness and identity as Earthlings was uniquely created to grow and spread unconditional love, equality, and unity!

We see it still is not resolved on your Earth plane.

Your people should ask how long they will discriminate.

Maybe, just maybe, discrimination will stop once the people learn through this conversation that each race is quite deliberate and perfect in their differences, and that all races share a history as intrepid explorers of the Universe with a binding mission to bring us together in acceptance, integration, inclusivity, and peace. Maybe this knowledge will begin to enlighten humankind to the truth that each race is to be respected as the

beloved starseeded descendants of the Enlightened Ones.

This would be the desired outcome, yes, and do we think this one set of words alone will enable this change? We do not, but we are pleased to contribute our wishes that your Earth people begin to be enlightened about this seeding and begin to understand differences for what they are—strengths.

Each seeding on your Earth plane brought skills and strengths and likelihoods of growth and success of a culture. As your Earth turned and your time continued, peoples came and went, struggled and succeeded, were overcome by Mother Nature or learned to work *with her* for survival and even successes above this, and others quietly succumbed to their challenges and did not prevail. There are lessons in each. There is no failure to be found but rather a need to regroup and try again in another format—this was done. Each of your people-groups have contributions to make in your world of today; each has beliefs and strengths and also challenges, and all contribute, when shared, to a strengthened society. This is the lesson.

The wide variety of languages that we have on Earth must also then have origins tied to the various starseeded peoples. Do our languages today still somewhat resemble the languages of the peoples from our starseed planets of origination?

Well this is a no-brainer to some while being a great conundrum to others. Do these divisions in looks and language bear resemblance to origins? We say they do, and they are remnants of the beginnings of diversity on your planet. We see it is not yet accepted in many of your locations, countries, and we ask how long does it take to assimilate those who contribute and happen to appear different? We say it is the source of so much upheaval in your civilization as a whole, with no need for it in this time and place. We wonder at it.

So, our variety of human races, or "people-groups" as you say, came from different peoples from various galaxies. However, were they all from galaxies within our Universe, or also from other Universes?

Ah yes, there were visitors from afar (other Universes) as well as from your galaxy. They do buzz about and visit and leave traces sometimes and none at others. When it is considered a possibility to spread good and knowledge of advanced ways, they have done so. It was not always the desired outcome, however, when less than hospitable inhabitants were encountered. Those were left untouched and sometimes approached at a later time with successful outcomes for all.

This whole "Planet Earth Project" depends on a certain place and presence, which we too

often take for granted, and yet, she is the hostess and platform.

For our people to feel a true kinship and connection to Earth we'll need to know why Earth should be considered *our* "Mother Earth" when she is not the planet from which we originated?

To adopt a homeland and call it so is the way of your people. One need not originate from a place to feel at home there. Knowing your Mother Earth supports your life and happiness is the basis for a relationship. At this time in your evolution there is no alternative. There will be, but this is not the question.

Pax, my dear, we are going to rock the boat—in a very good way, I think—on this intriguing topic of our evolution and its replacement with the truth of who we are.

I wonder, did our major religions and deities originate from the different planets from which we were starseeded? Or, did the peoples once here on Earth then form their own beliefs and deities?

Oh yes, the question of religious origin. Populations on Earth determined their own paths to follow in worship based upon experiences and beliefs of what or who protected them.

Some believed in nature, some in animals, and some in living people. As time went on and generations came and went, those beliefs grew and deepened and what began as a transfer of power—from a people to another for their belief that they were protected—grew to legend.

That these people were responsible for knowing the way and protecting themselves had been forgotten, and that power given over to another for worship. It is common amongst your people today, yes?

Yes.

While we have developed many differences in our religious beliefs, there are some references and experiences that many can relate to, I hope.

If you consider the ways of your aboriginal first peoples, this is how your Planet Earth does best. Everything has a soul, is their belief, whether plant or animal or rock or river or tree, everything has soul, and to treat each being in this way is to practice love and compassion for all. This is how to educate your people to protect Earth and her environment. For the people of your time to continue to flourish on Planet Earth, wisdom and guidance from advanced civilizations would be helpful, however, wisdom and guidance from your aboriginal peoples will be even more valuable to preserve what you have and repair Mother Earth where needed. You must look to the past to see the future ways.

Speaking of first peoples, of the many Starseeded Peoples from many other planets in

this galaxy and beyond, which people were the very first to arrive to Earth?

The First Peoples of your planet are here now and show themselves as aboriginals, and their people, and their people, are descended from the off-planet visitors who came and went and seeded populations around the globe.

There is common DNA to be found among people with no way of physical contact in those earliest days when travel was impossible beyond local inhabitant's areas.

Are the First Nations people of North America related from the same home planet of Starseed Origin to, say, the indigenous people of the Asian sub-continent of India, or are the African nations peoples related through Starseed Origin to the aboriginal Australian people; that kind of thing?

Oh yes this is the way of it. These continents split apart over time, eliminating ways of journeying from place to place other than by water. There have been treks far and wide and peoples were starseeded, planted as it were, and DNA can be and is noted today in its similarities among people spread far and wide. Gives new meaning to the term, distant cousin, yes?

It is the case that these "earlys" were seeded far and wide and cultures developed differently as a result of topography and climate. This was a given and these things still rule development in many geographical areas of your globe.

Yes, it was a common goal to develop Planet Earth as best it could be done to find another center of life and intelligence to add to those out there in the galaxy and further. Like you now send up to a space station as an artificial planet and place, people live there for extended periods as a test, so too was Earth used for this experiment.

That it has survived is surprising to some who watch and wait for the demise due to present massive growth of pollution and poisoning in all ways.

Who watches? Who are "those visitors among you from inter-stellar sources"? You used this sentence earlier and it sounds like a present-time happening. Are these interstellar visitors among us _now_?

Always, in one form or another, not always solid. We have stated they buzz by to monitor progress. Some will watch longer than others before departure.

When you say, "not always solid", does this indicate that interstellar visitors can be present among us in a form that is not seen or detected?

Well yes, they have this means of travel and being that is in thought form as well as solid. They may monitor progress on your Earth without being seen and they may also take form and participate at times.

Another way is akin to remote viewing and another is via thought-form communication and watching. There is choice. Each is designed to be not worrisome to your people and this is considerate, yes?

I'd say so.

There is no intention to be intrusive and yet there is intention to be watchful as they consider how to proceed with contact or not.

At present your Earth politicians, government, industry, and ordinary citizens are not sufficiently informed about extraterrestrials and their intentions to manage this contact without fear and aggression. Your watchers do not intend harm, nor do they intend anything other than communication. This would not be understood at this time, so they watch and wait—this is their reasoning behind the actions.

Do our ancient relatives who Starseeded us here care about us or are we just a disappointing experiment?

Now, it is not your ancient relatives caring at this time, but rather those continuing to buzz by to view progress. It is they who marvel at what once was pristine now being smoke and haze covered with air not breathable in many areas. It is they who are saddened.

Where have our ancient relatives gone? Why don't they check on us and on this "experiment" of putting many races together on one planet?

Well now, consider that ancient and still present are not always compatible. That they may have "gone on" is to be considered, and that those who still watch have taken up that mantle, is the case. Not all is forever in the Universe.

As those who seeded your Earth planet had and have great interest in the present and future of your Earth civilization, they also have interests elsewhere and sometimes tire of watching your people's nonauthentic, in their view, progress or lack thereof. And so, where do they go, you ask? Away to refresh themselves and place emphasis elsewhere where there could be positive outcomes and joy produced from the lessons they teach. It is not that they no longer believe in the future of Earth people to overcome their self-destructive tendencies, but rather that they tire of waiting.

So, your watchers have changed shift, as it were, and some go on to place their emphasis and talents elsewhere and replacements come to you in hopes of seeing a corner turned toward higher consciousness attainment leading to higher-consciousness living. Some come and some go; it is the way of it.

Your civilization has grown and flourished, then self-destructed and shrunk, and then the cycle repeats. Yours is not the first to begin down a path of corruption and self-interest, but it is doing so now. While many voices are now raised toward a resurgence of what came before in the way of aversion to these destructive lifestyles, they are in themselves not sufficient to the cause.

Who *can* help the cause?

Your current civilization has benefited for a long while now from the arrival of those star seeds, more recently the arrival of highly advanced thinkers, with conscience to match, are with you to lead the way on environmental and humanitarian improvements.

You see them, you hear them, and you wonder at the intensity of their leadership to change your planet for the better. They walk among you and will be responsible for positive change on a global basis. They speak to inform and change outdated thinking and inaction. They accept nothing less than action to make change to save Planet Earth, beginning now. You see and hear them, and they do not go away. It is their purpose in life, so we say listen and learn and act accordingly.

Were these "highly advanced thinkers" born in the here and now by human parents, reincarnated highly evolved souls? Or, are they true *aliens* to Earth?

Oh yes, these are the old souls, the wise ones who have determined that to reincarnate and return to your current world is their purpose now. They are born to human parents, entering the next stage of their evolution to return to Earth to teach; to show the way to wellness.

They bring integrity and knowledge of the ways forward to regain purity of heart for your people and purity of air and water, soil, and methods of resource management.

They are to be considered the wise-ones of your time.

The time of commercialism and disrespect is leaving, not quietly, but it cannot continue and expect the new leaders to emerge in those conditions.

Nowadays, there are many people who speak on the environmental crisis in depth and with passion—and many of them are children or young adults who are so incredibly well educated and well spoken.

They make their thoughts and voices heard, their circles of influence broaden, and the impact is felt. They are the forerunners of the next big change and pave the way by removing from power the corrupt. They do this by being vocal in their concerns and speaking of the inconsistencies, of mankind's inhumanity to mankind, high-level corruption, and the collusion that currently runs rampant in the management of companies and countries. The facts will be heard—the proponents exposed, and the startling outcomes witnessed. People formerly with heads positioned firmly in the sand emerge, horrified, and pledge to make the necessary changes in their own spheres of influence. The ripple effect is felt, and the positive energy created by the many supports in their decision to follow and create their own changes.

They bring intention and knowledge and attitude and will not be unheard on issues of colossal import to your Planet Earth. You see them and hear them and wonder at their level of knowledge, passion, and expertise.

It is their determination that the leaders of today do not have the understanding of the "big picture" and see the resulting demise of the health of your planet. You will see them being leaders from an early age, yes, and seemingly knowing how to make a difference in your world, whether it be climate change or politics or humanitarian issues. It is they who bring solutions and more, showing the way to a future of peace and wellness for all.

We've taken in a lot of new information and perhaps it's time for a pause of reflection. To recap, you've confirmed that we did not originate from Planet Earth, Bigfoot is real, and there are advanced thinkers among our people who will lead in global wellness.

This is all *very* exciting!

You also said, "Yours is not the first to begin down a path of corruption and self-interest,

but it is doing so now." It's compelling to hear that our civilization is not the first to begin down a path of corruption and self-interest. In terms of the peoples of those other planets that went down the path of destruction, was monetary gain the driving force for these ways of self-interest?

Indeed, our reference here is to *early civilizations on Planet Earth.*

There have been many powerful and advanced civilizations. From the Roman Empire to Aztec, there were numerous that rose, prospered, and then fell. It is now awaited that your consciousness-raising trends will flow in the direction of higher evolution and this time your civilization will continue to evolve and thrive in peace and harmony.

A world of no warring and corruption in future, no greed and territorial attitude of control and power grab—how long does it take for this to become the way of your world? Generations will pass on the journey to this higher functioning.

Is it now known that this is to be the goal? We say it is and as alternatives present, they will be considered, but overall wellness comes. As your people view the opposite of this, they see the darkness of the energy created and sustained and want no part of it going forward. This darkness resides within your political powers. It is not new in your world history but is to be removed from the reality of your world.

Has there ever been a planet destroyed by its human occupants, whereby the whole planet was lost? Or, is Earth the only planet being harmed (or that has been destroyed) by its people?

No other planets destroyed by its people, not so, but destroyed by natural phenomena in their solar system, it happens.

Now it is the case that this has become reality on Planet Earth.

On the faraway planets from which all varieties of people *originated*, how did *those* people develop? Was it an evolution of life from single-cell organisms all the way up to primates and so on? Or, is there some other magical creation way that you can tell us about?

Magic indeed, and this is the way of it.

Do not think that all things began with single-cell organisms for they did not necessarily and our ability to describe the journey from there to today is limited to what you need to understand, and that is that awareness and creation come together to plant what is needed, where needed, and suited for that specific purpose. Rather like a custom build or a purpose-specific build—we leave that thought.

Pax, that's a pretty big announcement to just mention in passing. May you please tell us a bit more about how life creation works?

It has been the way through your time that as there is a need, so is there a solution. This accounts for developments and surprise findings in all ways of your civilization as your technology advances exponentially. It brings your people forward in thinking and growing intellectually and becoming curious and acting upon their questions to find answers, noting problems and finding solutions.

As intellect grows, so does civilization.

If traced right back to the beginning of the beginning, did all peoples (from all planets, in all galaxies; everywhere) come from one original planet and peoples?

And where is that beginning it is asked? Was it in one place and time or did beginnings become on many levels and in many locations simultaneously?

Obviously, the latter. I know now how you nicely wrap the answer in a question and ask us to come to it on our own.

It is a thought that scholars wrestle with and bring interesting theories to the fore. We suggest the lingering result of a sparking of interest in *being*: was it an idea and an episode of adventure amongst those creating, those who could create, that which was creation in waiting?

Galaxies had their identities and wisdoms and the source managed to be the wisdom and the identity; the creator.

Who are "those creating, those who could create"?

The source of all, the God-energy, the *being*, and beings who did and do still and will continue—there is that energy overall—encompassing and enveloping and wise.

Does each galaxy have a creator?

It is not the case that there are lines of creators responsible for their portions of the Universe. This remains mystical and thought-provoking for some, but *above all* (no pun intended) is the strength of wisdom and Spirit.

Very cute, Pax, very cute.
"*Above all*, the God-energy,"—however, creators of any kind are not deities, right?

Not deities and no need to be considered such. It is the way of creation, then and now, it is what it is.

Chapter Three

Earth Mysteries Revealed

*I*t's a rare opportunity to be having a dialog with the God being. I'd like to take the opportunity to talk about some of our legends and folklore.

We referred to our self as God being, yes, and it was intended to describe how Earth people may think of our type of energy, our type of essence if you will.

There are many references that do not use the word God. You would not use the term Allah or Krishna for the same reason that using "God" for us causes disruption in the Christian psyche. We suggest not using this term now and in place of it use Divine Source, Divine Wisdom, Divine Guidance or the like.

Yes, we spoke about the importance of inclusivity. Thank you for the reminder.

Let's now start with the mysterious events that have occurred—*especially historically more so than today*—**within the area called the Bermuda Triangle located in the western part of the North Atlantic Ocean, such as the disappearance of ships and aircraft.**

Ah yes, this is a not-charmed area of your world that has seen its share of disaster. Why is this, you ask? Well, we are here to say it is a place of deep, underground caverns, which harbor the minerals that interfere with navigation now and far back into your history. These elements are not of the area; they were brought for a purpose.

Brought by whom?

These underground caverns have been home to underwater UFO bases and now not occupied, although will be again. With what was there, and remains in place, the magnetics are too powerful to override by commercial navigation of the time. These elements which cause magnetic interference are responsible for far more than interruption to navigation.

Like what? What else are these underground caverns responsible for?

Responsible for the good and useful means of recharging the craft that use the base—it is the overarching reason for the creation of the base. What serves as good for the visitors has created havoc to marine and air travelers, and with combined resources may be amended to reduce the potential of risk for Earth people. We can speak more to this in time.

So, these minerals are not natural to the Earth?

Not natural to the Earth planet. These aspects of the underwater base were included in materials relied upon for their specific purpose and transported with ETs as necessary materials.

What are these minerals that cause magnetic interference for our navigation systems yet are useful to recharge extraterrestrial spacecraft?

As margins of error go, these products of the future will not be named here as references will be negated. Suffice it to say that what was and will be again is not known to your science. When the day comes for awareness; all is revealed.

How long ago did ETs occupy these caverns?

Used as underwater bases for travel and visitation *throughout Earth history*, from time to time recharging was initiated there of flight craft. You will understand the base was a purpose-built creation and all aspects of it were brought to the site from off-planet.

It was set up for a specific purpose and operated for the specified time required, after which left in place for future use.

How fascinating. I guess this base goes way back to the initial starseeding of Earth. Given this, these extraterrestrials must certainly feel that they have both a purpose and a right, *perhaps even an obligation*, to occupy such a base at will.

Protection of this area has been foremost in the minds of those watching over it and this will not change.

To be clear, who "watches over" the Bermuda Triangle? (Don't mind me while I shake my head to ring-in this news.)

Those who created the base to suit their needs of travel and visitation watch to ensure it remains untouched. Nothing is of monetary value to Earth people; simply a need to maintain viability of the area for future use. While there is a need for this base, it is to be as it was left and as it is intended— this is the protection.

Can anything be done to make this area safe for ships and planes in present time?

We must say that this present situation of restricted access will continue, and it is best to avoid the area if possible. Otherwise, there are precautions to take which can make a difference.

What kind of precautions?

We say that respecting Mother Earth and her depths is a beginning, and asking for her protection, as mariners do, when passing through challenging weather and locations, is the way. While it is the off-planet creators of these bases who watch, it is heard, by them, that safe-passage is requested through air and water.

There are times when it appears peaceful, this area, and other times when watchfulness steps up to a high level and resulting mysteries occur. They are not mysteries to us, and to your people we say have respect when passing through, ask for permission to do so, much like you should respect the traditional territories of your First Nations peoples. This is a novel idea for your people, but one that is ancient and works. When you respect another's territory and ask permission to pass through, that permission is historically granted when peaceful intentions exist. That no people live in that area does not negate the need for respect of the associated elements, those who create and those who visit.

You've said that the ETs have left, for now, so from whom do we need to ask for permission?

Mother Earth, as explained above in precautions.

And, this ET base will again be occupied?

It will, and until that time there will be relative peace there regarding those ships and planes traversing the waters and skies.

Remain peaceful in intent, speak it and place the blessings on your people and craft—this explains the intention and is a good idea at any time, yes?

Yes, I suppose it is.

This is not the only Earth location of such a base, although has resulted in notoriety of the area through no intention of the visitors. In other locations the coming and going is less of an attention-getter and no disruptions caused in nature or Earth travel.

Really? In what other places on Earth were there similar ET bases?

Oh well now, this is an interesting story as there were and are similar bases. At present, in your time, there are on the North American west coast and near Venezuela as well as in the Northern areas of your globe. There are more but less frequented and harbor nothing that interrupts travel on your planet at this time.

It is purely for the protection of the bases that quiet is kept about their locations, although those residing close do know of their presence as the ships come and go and are noticed. It is a neighborly thing to do, this allowing each to live their lives without interference—like across a fence you know others are there in the process of living lives differently, but friendly allowances for others prevails. This is the attitude of the visitors and of those who see and feel and know their presence and remain quiet and supportive. Live and let live, yes?

Indeed, and let me just go over that: there are, still at this time, *occupied* ET bases on Earth?

Occupied for brief periods of time as the visitors come, monitor and leave—this is their way.

More than you know, it is their wish for peace and harmony around your globe and their visitations show them it is not the way for you, and they depart once again. The day will come when there is change and that is into your future, meanwhile they bring harmony and good intentions only. Allow it.

Pax, what is a wormhole in space?

For the storage of worms?

Ha! You're quite the character sometimes. But, for real, what's a wormhole in space?

In all of the galaxy there are many anomalies and one is the ability to move from place to place in time without effort and without intention, always. It is a time and place and a movement toward another experience that defies logic and brings awe to those attempting to dissect it to understand the step-by-step action of it. Release this and allow it to become for you when the time is right.

Got it: a wormhole is a space-travel highway of sorts, kind of like an intergalactic high-speed train. Now, to why I asked about wormholes...

Some of our current-day pilots, even military pilots, have reported a wormhole-like vortex in the airspace within the area called the Bermuda Triangle. Here's an example: I recently watched a documentary featuring a couple of pilots who said that they had been pulled into a tunnel vortex, yet with great effort they managed to travel through it before it closed behind them. They safely landed at their destination, although ahead of schedule and had used less fuel than the flight should have consumed.

Is there such a "wormhole" in the airspace of the Bermuda Triangle?

Your pilots have experienced this, and we say it is. We clarify that this vortex is a place where entry into another time is possible, and that they, in this example given, landed safely at their chosen destination is example of intention. It was their choice to touch down where they planned, and so it was.

Did ETs create this time-vortex? Is it some-how involved in the protection of the ET base that you spoke of? And, are there other time-vortexes in our Earth atmosphere?

Throughout your time and space there are por-tals to other dimensions—always have been—and they account for the disappearance of ships at sea and airplanes above. It is the way of the Universe that these cracks in spacetime exist and travelers find themselves other than where they anticipated being. These are dis-associated with the magnetics previously mentioned and not a result of closeness to undersea ET bases. Time warps are and always have been, and a mystery to you they remain.

Ah, so they're a natural phenomenon.

You've given us much to think about. Before we leave this topic, I'd like to ask about the disap-pearance of the female aviator Amelia Earhart. She disappeared in the central Pacific Ocean, perhaps in the vicinity of the Bermuda Triangle, while in flight on the second of July 1937. There has been much speculation on her disappearance. People want to know if she simply crashed and died (if so, why?) or did she survive for a time.

So, what really happened to Amelia Earhart, her flight navigator Fred Noonan, and her shiny Lockheed Model 10-E Electra craft? What hap-pened that day? What went wrong? Was her air-craft affected by the magnetic minerals of which

you spoke? Did she crash yet survive on an island somewhere? Did her aircraft travel through a portal of sorts and end up elsewhere?

Indeed, she flew into a vortex that took her safely into another dimension. It is a continuation of the mystique that surrounds her and her flight and that her aircraft has never been found is a part of this. She was an adventuress and did not dispute what she experienced when it began—she allowed the playing out of the steps that took her into and through the tunnel and deposited her into another place in time.

As she was prepared in her heart for all adventures that came her way, she was not fearful of what she began to experience in this portion of her journey. She was an explorer and allowed this experience to become her next reality. She was chosen. She accepted the challenge and the rest, as they say, is history.

Amelia Earhart, her aircraft, and companion went through a time-vortex to another time dimension! This—all of this—is the makings of a great movie. And, here, another showstopper.

She felt the calling to higher adventure, spiritually, and while she was flying high and, in her mind, touching the face of God, she became exhilarated by the feeling of closeness to the Universe when she came near to the vortex.

In some way she knew there was opportunity to further explore the unknown, and when presented with it she continued on into it.

The Universe provides what the soul craves.

What time-era did they come out into? Was it earlier or later in our history to 1937?

The era, the wrinkle in time, the landing place, the folding into a new reality for this aircraft and passengers is and will remain a mystery for your people. That there always is a defining time and place for all things is not the case.

As this unfolds it will be shown that a space-time adventure continues as this adventuress continues her explorations in another dimension where all flight is possible and continues as desired. There is no beginning or end and there is no definitive flight plan—it is a time-free zone she encounters and enjoys.

Fly free and dream on, the wish of many is hers.

What a beautiful thought for us to hold.

Now, I'd like to ask you about the sunken continents of Atlantis and Lemuria—these lost civilizations greatly interest me. What do you know of them?

Much like Sodom and Gomorrah, there are times when what has gone wrong has gone so wrong that the end result is annihilation, and this was a case of self-destruction. These civilizations had much in common and much to offer. They also had the choice between good and evil. It was the case that the planet, at those times, also underwent a great change from within and it resulted in a climate change type cataclysmic event not fully understood, but suffice it to say, it was a result of the energy emanating from each.

Were there other continents on Earth that are now sunken?

Looking beneath the sea for signs of life will show numerous cities now submerged due to the rising of sea levels, not uncommon. Lost continents are another story.

There are not what you think of as continents imbedded on the sea floor. There have been cataclysmic earth shakings that resulted in the breaking away of pieces of coastal areas and those are hard to identify. It is the case that perusing the ocean's floor turns up much but not this.

Your civilizations of past are most often to be found beneath the sand and soil of your planet. The passage of time has resulted in a diminishing of civilization and abandonment of those civilization's homelands and residences. As growth comes again to these areas it has been common to resurrect what can be and build over what cannot to the extent that antiquities grow, one upon the other in some places, and to go straight down is the way to find history. Not so under water.

In time the cities of North America will suffer the same fate if your world does not adopt cleaner living policies.

You are not immune from the wrath of Mother Nature.

Let's briefly touch back on Sodom and Gomorrah because you bring it up. You've used the example as a parallel to the self-destruction of the two continents—Lemuria and Atlantis— in the sense of energetic impacts resulting from wrongs of dark intentions and actions such as hatred, warring, disrespect to nature, and more. However, let's talk about it further because our people can so easily get things wrong. (It's one of our bad habits.)

Sodom and Gomorrah were cities of antiquity that were mentioned in the Christian Bible, the Hebrew Bible, and the Islamic Quran. The general lesson was that the peoples there had committed great sins—some versions of the story point to acts of homosexuality—and therefore the cities were destroyed by the wrath of the deity that corresponds to each religious tradition. (*I pause here to take a deep breath at what seems so archaic and backwards thinking.*) Let's please clarify the example of the Sodom and Gomorrah story as it relates to the fate of the sunken continents of Lemuria and Atlantis.

If you refer to the demise of these two civilizations, yes, they contributed to their implosion:
turmoil and hate and greed and darkness of energy
settling, the soil under them gave way to opening
and the rest is history.

Do you know your world is looking in that direction now? Although, we see change coming to you
to offset the same fate.

**May we clear up some ideas about homosexu-
ality? Painfully, it still seems to be a topic of division and debate for some people. We've already
mentioned it so we might as well get some insight
from the Spirit World on this.**

What is it you wish to ask? If it is about equality
and acceptance and mutual respect, then of course
there should be all this and more shown from one
individual to another despite differences. This is not
new, but it is still treated as sub-species and shameful.

The shame is in not accepting each individual for
who they are.

A part of healing all on your planet is finding total
acceptance for life on Earth in all forms. To accept those
with differences in makeup is to grow and evolve, and
to not do so is to become stuck in a judgmental place
where no amount of speaking of the need to will result
in people accepting others with differences.

As an extension of this, that judgmental nature
makes for a smaller world for individuals so afflicted
and they continue to cycle down into a smaller self

instead of growing and accepting and spreading this sense of love to all.

Very good insights. Profound. Now I feel we can return to our conversation about Earth's lost continents. The peoples from the advanced civilization of Lemuria: are any still around today, perhaps hidden around or inside Mount Shasta, California, as our legends say?

An interesting theory, this is, but what resides within Mount Shasta is rock and more rock. It is a sacred space to the indigenous peoples of the area and—as part of their traditional territory—it is blessed with some protection. Legends are self-perpetuating, yes?

I've read that highly evolved civilizations keep knowledge of Earth's true history on some sort of crystal discs—is this true?

Crystal discs are mythology for humankind, but one not too far from truth of the interstellar visitors' way of recording history, rather like a logbook of centuries.

Within there will be entries reflecting travel and visits and results, and much like Akashic records, will not be accessed by the many.

Thanks to our Internet, I found this on Wikipedia: "The Akashic records are a

compendium of all human events, thoughts, words, emotions, and intent ever to have occurred in the past, present, or future. They are believed by theosophists to be encoded in a non-physical plane of existence known as the etheric plane."

In further researching Akashic records, I've learned that these are also referred to as "white noise extraction systems" and are described as the standing energy waves in spacetime containing all history and all events in all times that ever existed to date.

The Universe must have a reason for such a perfectly designed record system, and someone *must* be able to access these. How can we access the Akashic records?

Ah yes, these records can be accessed by anyone with high spiritual interest and training and powers. It is through the work of Spirit that the door swings open to this hall of records and access is given. You are to consult your Higher Self and whether in meditation or other practices, consider this as a desire. Attaching the intention to use this information for the highest and best good of all, you may move forward.

I will practice this for the highest and best good of all.

Are there any historical and tangible records left specifically from the people of Lemuria?

That would be unlikely, but we can say the search continues and more is to be known when exploration is further enabled.

And what about Atlantis: does any evidence of this continent still exist, if we knew where to look?

There are those who know where to look and believe they are finding ruins they attribute to Atlantis. Is it, is it not? Time will tell as more and deeper examination of remnants is enabled.

Dedication to this cause continues and in your soon time will be interpretation of the findings with what some deem is proof of the existence and demise of Atlantean civilization.

Are there subterranean cities on this planet?

If you ask about living cities, then it is not the case. If you ask about remains of previous civilizations, then yes, very much, as over time the seas have risen, and coastal inhabitants and villages have been taken by the tides. It is a repeating event now on your planet as the seas again rise and those nearby are and will be impacted by loss of land and lifestyle. History repeats itself in climate change, ice ages come and go, warming and cooling cycles, and life goes on. It can be moderated, as your people now think can be done, and time will show it can if attention is paid to the cleaning of your natural resources and protection from future polluting.

Oh, here's another fascinating (to us) question. What happened to the Mayans? The archeological and anthropological evidence shows a people who were there one minute, so to speak, and gone the next. Their cities were abandoned, and no sign of their peoples turns up elsewhere or again. It is said that they disappeared. Did they just "rapture-out" to another world or another dimension like some of us wonder? And, what's the significance of the much-discussed Mayan Calendar and their ties to the stars?

We are here to report that the teleportation of the Mayan peoples took place when their calendar year ended—abruptly but planned evacuation as it were.

Why did they do this, you ask? Theirs had been a civilization of great worship and god-practices and preparation for their ascension in many ways. They had a plan to rise to the epitome of their abilities, do their finest work in growing their civilization to its highest performance level, and then moving on to another home base. They were advanced in their ways and determined to not languish in that one place when it was felt their work there was done.

And so it was that they departed as they had arrived, quietly and with intention.

Well, blow me over with a feather.

Pax, what was the purpose of the Mayan calendar going all the way to the twenty-first of December of the year 2012 when the Mayans successfully teleported off-planet so very many years earlier?

Well this is an interesting philosophical question of your time, yes.

The end of that calendar, dated as it was, indicated a belief at the time that the Universe would be in turmoil and the Planet Earth would catapult out and away from the galaxy. It was the astronomers of the time who set up this belief based on their study of the skies, movements they saw, and intentions of theirs to be at the forefront of exploration of space, from the safety of their cities, while informing the masses through their calendar that plans would be made to evacuate what they thought of as a doomed planet.

Did they think life could be sustained while Earth was hurtling through space in an uncontrolled manner? No, they did not, and therefore quietly prepared to teach the population of the intent to remove themselves from harm. Stated in that way it seemed a natural extension of their civilization to relocate for safety and take their wisdoms, customs, and advanced technology with them to begin again elsewhere. This was accomplished at a time of their choice, the end of calendar date being so far in future their departure could come when they were prepared and well within the calendar deadline.

What was the significance of that precise date of the twenty-first of December of the year 2012?

It was a mathematical equation used to arrive at the numbers as they added in their calendar to a total representing success and higher functioning of the endeavor to relocate. Mathematics was the basis, as it was for much in this civilization.

It is reported that about forty percent of Guatemala's fourteen million people are of Mayan decent. Is this correct; did a portion of the Mayans stay behind?

There are always dissenters to any rule and sure enough, there were those who chose the terra firma they knew over that they did not, so branched out to nearby places to await the departure of their countrymen. They stayed and that is the choice that proved a good one for many. They took their culture with them and contributed to their adopted homeland. What you have today is a melding of cultures and history and if you check DNA you will find interesting mix of mysteries.

Yes, mysteries, and this will show a mix of *other* peoples—we say no more at this time.

DNA and genealogy are easily tested nowadays. Once news of a mystery waiting to be uncovered is out, I'm sure we'll soon begin to

find out about the mix of other peoples. To be continued!

As we're all very interested, what are the Mayans doing these days (those Mayans who teleported out, that is)?

They went far and fast and happily established themselves well onto a hospitable homeland and began their worship and continuation of their excelling in all things. They brought science and astronomy and astrology and healing, of course, and created a hierarchy as they grew into the formidable and highly functioning society they demand. They are outside of your range now but will make themselves known again in time.

We will look forward to the reunion.

This is going to be a wild and fun conversation for many people, and many others will have a very hard time believing in extraterrestrial beings and peoples who travel from planet to planet. What should be considered, however, is the impressive number of astronauts who believe in ETs and who have reported UFOs and other happenings that, to them, can only be explained by the existence of intelligent life outside of our world.

American astronaut, Buzz Aldrin, said this about the moon of Mars: "There's a monolith there. When people find out about that they're going to say, 'Who put that there? Who put that there?'"

Pax, is there a monolith (a large piece of placed rock or structure built as a monument or building) on the moon of Mars? And, who put it there?

To not doubt the word of one who has seen is best, and yes, it is to appear not as a naturally made creation.

How does this appear in a place not seemingly visited in past? Who is to say it was not visited in the past? The past, as you think of it, is quite recent as opposed to the past in terms of galaxies and moons and history of those from outer-ports of advanced life. So, let us inform that some carvings appear to have been planted, *and were*, and it is their anomaly that garners attention.

It is there for wonder and it is there for a statement, somewhat like planting a flag for people of your time. We say the "who" is not as important as the "why" in this case. Suffice it to say the visitors to that place determined it to be a meeting place and not a staying in place. This marker indicated so to those who followed.

Fascinating, to say the least. Dr. Aldrin might be gratified to be validated after all of these years.
And, is there anything extraterrestrial in creation about Ayers Rock in Australia? Called Uluru by indigenous aboriginal Australians, this sandstone monolith dramatically sticks out in an otherwise flat landscape and is sacred to the

aboriginals. Is there something interesting to know about it?

Sacred it is and sacred it has always been as a piece of inner earth thrust upward to arrive in that position of no return to below. As that continent flexed and shook and fractured in spots, that which was beneath the surface and wanting to decrease pressure was allowed to escape the darkness and appear to the native inhabitants but there were none present at that time. This came later and the history is recorded to include this as a draw, a pilgrimage for those who, in wonder, came to look and touch and climb to the top. Drawings and carvings appeared to record these events and the belief that Mother Earth had provided a Goddess rock for worship began.

The sacred site gave and gives hope and belief to the indigenous peoples that something greater than themselves exists in their place and time. It is now reverting to sacred trust and being held away from the ravages of unlimited and unwise visitors who damage and deface this wonder of nature.

Talking about "earth thrust" makes me think of the Earth's *crust*: is it thinning as some scientists say? If so, why?

It is the case that Earth's crust thins and recovers through time with warming and cooling and ice ages and heat waves—it remains flexible. Now it is in a period of constriction once again. Nothing in nature is rigid. Periods of growth and periods of decline in areas of your Earth peoples have been the way through history. It is and it will be and is not to be feared as the end of anything—it is a cycle.

What do periods of growth and decline in areas of our Earth peoples have to do with the thinning of the Earth's crust? Are we somehow controlling the Earth's geological cycles?

Well yes, and it is the case that "areas" refers to geographical areas where, over time, natural as well as unnatural events have occurred. It is these warming and cooling periods that make the change, and these are largely created by Earth population. Some are and some are not, and this is the way of it.

As cycles go on your Earth plane and in your history, climate has changed to warm and again to cool, cataclysmic events in nature have occurred and nothing has been constant, nor will it be going forward. Every action has a reaction and here it is in view.

Just know that your people are active, and Earth is largely passive, and you affect your future on Planet Earth.

Let's talk about our population and the bearing limit of our planet. Do advanced civilizations limit their population somehow? What advice do you have for us on this sensitive topic?

Ah yes, sensitive it is, for controlling population growth is not always wise. While some civilizations, countries now on your planet have done so; it was released as a law after a period of time. The people won't stand for it and other means must be found.

Wars and pestilence were means of reducing populations in past; neither of which are wanted in your current time, but the warring continues on parts of the globe and pestilence can be a current-day threat as is pollution and drugs, all of which reduce populations. There are self-governing means of population control such as birth control, widely used in some places and not in others.

We say the overall means of controlling population—as on other planets and in other civilizations—has been wisdom. Those cultures function at a higher vibratory level and understand the ways of peace and love. They do not war and they do not function in hate or anything negative. Their way of going is to find peace and share peace and small communities of intellectual souls prevail. It is not a rule of law, but rather a self-imposed wish to focus on self-awareness and evolution, on furthering their goal of enlightenment, which requires inner focus. Are they self-centered; we say yes in the best possible way. The path to enlightenment is theirs.

Pax, I have so many questions about life, Earth, space. For instance—what is a black hole in space? And what is its purpose?

A black hole is a repository for what comes by and is destined for other places and other uses.

It is the case that a balance is created here, and there is no end-place for the space debris now, but black holes could be a vacuum for what your people have left and describe as "space junk". You aren't really there yet and debris is your legacy already—why do we think your colonization of another planet is a good thing for your Earth? It is to become yet another litter location for your people if minds and hearts do not change on this topic. Why is it you find it necessary to discard and forget about it? Why is lack of planning for resources no longer needed, and still reality? Do you not grow with your forward motion in life? We say it is to be the downfall of your intentions to relocate and revive civilization.

We are here to advise that the mysteries of space are to remain so for as long as needed to entice your people to learn and explore and consider themselves in a very good place, so good, in fact, that mind-sets change and cleanup in earnest of Planet Earth accelerates.

I suppose that our space travel does include the steady leaving-behind of space litter such as discarded satellites and rocket stages.

There are others above who watch and are not pleased. As they buzz by to observe, they also must carefully plan their route so as to avoid banging up against your litter—for shame people, clean up your own place before thinking of how to leave your footprint elsewhere.

Infinity is where it ends and there is no end to infinity, yes?

I'm inferring that black holes are part of that infinity: everything that comes by is accumulated and stored for a while, and eventually whatever is collected in that vacuum goes—where?

Do your scientists understand that what goes in will come out elsewhere?

Where? **Where does all the matter go that is sucked in?**

This is for future consideration, yes, and for now it is to be understood that the Black Hole is the repository for what will appear elsewhere, in time. Where it goes is where it will go and that is to be.

What we can share is that it will burst, yes, for it will fill and like a volcano, spew contents up and out and through and around and down. It would be best to be elsewhere when this occurs, except that the contents will end up "elsewhere", but it will come as a welcome event. No more shall we share at this time, other than to divulge that what is in and comes out form building blocks for future civilizations on future colonies. All good, it is said.

With this— "What is in and comes out form building blocks for future civilizations on future colonies"—you just handed Steven Spielberg his next movie plot!

While our space junk is likely useless to interstellar colonies (after all, space junk is just garbage), perhaps black holes can be a delivery portal. Perhaps we could send a message through a black-hole-delivery-system. Could this be possible? Let's say that we filled a space-tight capsule with messages, pictures, and drawings—could it potentially reach those inhabitants of a space colony?

Well this is an interesting consideration. Not the intended purpose or highest use for the black hole as we know it, but as things go in, they will come out. Although, to aim for a specific end spot would be an exercise in futility. We used the term "spew", and that doesn't come with specific aiming capability. Perhaps the use in this manner can be attained with fine-tuning, and why not consider that a next stage development. All is possible in time and change is to be considered good and constructive and exciting, too.

So, a black hole is a holding place and one day it erupts like a volcano. To be clear, the stuff that is sucked in comes out elsewhere, like through a tunnel?

It has been stated that what goes in comes out elsewhere, and it could and would be random: that elsewhere. So, don't be between one place and the other when it happens. This is a dramatization but not completely as there will be space debris in motion.

Is there plot and plan for this action? We say not, and is there an ideal outcome of this action? Possibly. And what is to be the end result of this action? Now it is to be questioned and conjured and considered and not experienced or clarified for many turns of your Earth planet in another spacetime orbit. For now, it is a vast idea of infinite possibility.

When you spoke about our Starseeded Origins and the starseeded primates, you mentioned "a ship full of monkeys"—perhaps a reference to Noah's Ark. Was there really a guy named Noah, who, as the biblical story goes, built a huge ark and filled it with two of each species to save them from a great flood that destroyed the world as they knew it at that time?

It's a good story, yes? It is the case that writings from early times, as they have been edited and added to and translated into many languages, have become warped and exaggerated and diminished and generally changed to suit the translator or religions involved in the writings. We say to take all lessons with thought and filters and adopt those that feel right on a personal basis. Was there a giant boat— yes. And were there two of each species on the Earth planet—not likely, but there were many, and perhaps the two of everything refers to two of all that were known at the time. Some stories become embellished over time and the basis for this is sound but the story as it appears today includes the growth of the animal numbers to proportions not based on reality. But never mind, we say the lesson is there and the intention was good. Not all is non-fiction.

Pax, I've been meaning to ask you: who designed and built the Great Pyramids of Egypt? Even today, our best architects, physicists, and mathematicians can't figure out the mysteries of the building of these structures and their mind-boggling design. Were the pyramids designed by the locals (the people of that area and of that time) or are they the works of extraterrestrial visitors from advanced civilizations? And, who did the building labor—was it slave labor? How did the monstrous size stones get moved through the desert? What technology made that possible?

This is quite the conversation on your Earth plane, and the reality is those extraterrestrial visitors we speak of, those who buzz by from other galaxies to follow-up on Earth peoples' progress, were the advanced knowledge responsible.

It is the case that those who seeded civilization continued to monitor, and in their advanced technological development, it was a simplistic way of building they shared. Physics was well understood, obviously, as they built interstellar capable ships for travel, and they contributed their knowledge to those who accepted.

The movement of building materials was aided by some movement of thought: the intention of moving, teleportation if you will, is the way. As travel from place to place by teleportation is, so is the way to manage large-scale movement of stone. It is a dissolution of plasma in one place and reassembly in another. As your Earth saying goes, it's not rocket science. This is no different than dissolving clouds or creating any number of realities using the mind-power.

Is this how the stones of the Stonehenge circle in England were moved? Our physicists are still stuck on this one, too. It is said by our anthropologists that Stonehenge was built in six stages during the transition from the Neolithic Period (the New Stone Age) to the Bronze Age. It would seem to me that if the stones were moved by highly evolved and enlightened interstellar visitors using thought power, then well, they could have moved them much quicker than that! May you please help us to correct history here and enlighten us to when and why Stonehenge was built?

Gathering for worship has been the incentive for creation of structures such as this monument, and the peoples of the various times came with differing reasons and levels of intention for such a build. While the helpers from afar had capabilities surpassing those of the local inhabitants, they offered what was wanted and needed at the time. If the people wanted a box, they were not given a skyscraper as they would not have known what to do with one.

The evolution of this monument, as with others from early Earth times, came as awareness grew and knowledge grew to match it and the desired end-result was shown. One step at a time.

What is the structure beneath Stonehenge?

What is beneath is more of the same. Although, it will not be excavated, on that space, if so, it would show another but smaller circle. There have been circles in place for centuries and the numbers of those yet undiscovered is large. The worship and giving thanks for their gifts and abundance is the key for the build and the use of such places. To observe lunar cycles and star movements to be aware of the sun and moon, and to time their activities with these rotations was also key. The people of that time and place worshipped and gave thanks for what they had, planned and hoped for additional abundance of crops and lifestyles, and made it a point to show this gratitude daily. When gathering at monuments such as this for special occasions in the lunar calendar, there was heightened awareness of the power of the stars and planets, of the sun and moon, and humility and gratitude were the overriding feelings of the time. This is something that could be emulated in some aspects of your today society.

A daily practice of gratitude is a solid recommendation and is advised by just about every best-life coach and inspirational speaker of today. What is it about gratitude that is so important and powerful?

It is attraction of more to be grateful for.

You know that the laws of life say that what you think about you attract, well, when you are positive and grateful and thankful for the abundance in your lives, you live in a state of grace that is emphasized each time you share your gratitudes with the Universe. You become charmed and a target and magnet for continued abundance and it is a never-ending circle of joy.

To think the bliss and live the bliss and attract the bliss—a natural cycle in life—it is within you to create for yourself.

Charmed is a good way to think of this: lucky or happy as though protected by magic. I also like the description of "a never-ending circle of joy". Gratitude is a generator of more to be grateful for.

Switching gears, another item of speculation is polar axis swap. In the Earth's history, has there ever been a swapping of the poles and the axis of rotation of the Earth?

Not in the way you would think of it, no, and it is the case that the shifts in energy around the globe have been many and varied. Moving forward you will see the continued growth and change, as this is the way throughout your history. There is no need to fear this as your planet always recovers and recharges and restores herself to rightness.

Are you saying that there will never be a future cataclysmic Earth pole shift?

No need to consider this as possibility. What you do need to consider is protection of all of your nature as it roots your planet in the security of future wellness.

What triggered the last ice age?

Ice ages have come and gone throughout history and are often thought of as cataclysmic when in reality they are Earth's way of regrouping and beginning fresh with flora and fauna and purity of air and water. Rapid cooling of the atmosphere due to seasonal change, and by this is meant seasons comprised of thousands of years. It is a flow of air, atmospheric pressures, and change that originate far from your Earth.

The causation of our ice ages is "atmospheric pressures and change that originate far from your Earth"—wow.

This includes wholesale change on many stars and planets and comes from unknown-to-you source. It continues through time and space and is just the way of it.

This is fascinating: the Universe is holistic!
And, are *we* affecting Earth's poles and our magnetosphere?

All you do on and to your Planet Earth affects some aspect of it.

Withdraw from injuring the underground with explosions to enable fossil fuel extraction and withdraw from injuring the atmosphere with gasses and pollution and nuclear testing.

Is the danger of nuclear fallout or meltdown just too risky to pursue nuclear power? (*We must scare the pants off of our interstellar visitors!*)

This has its uses and positive features in the right hands of science, but you have world leaders who are demented and consider the use of this power as their own to threaten others into submission. It is a danger to your population to have this as a reality and a tool of warring people.

"World leaders who are demented." (Kinda funny, but not funny.)

Do not think that what you do is isolated—like ripples on the water these actions spread their negativity far and wide. Your people have concerns but feel disempowered to make change on a large scale.

We shall talk of this further—empowerment is a right for all.

I look forward to that discussion.

Scientists today are identifying a drift in the Earth's spin axis; therefore, magnetic north has moved. It has shifted so much so that they had to do an emergency update to the World Magnetic Model and GPS, yet no one can entirely explain the cause of the shift. Why is Earth's axis shifting?

A shift of this magnitude is not abnormal, and the existence and movement of stars and planets tends to be fluid rather than fixed forever. There is spin and change—Earth events that bring massive change to parts of your globe and affect the health of your planet—and the likelihood of future change and the intellectual community fears this. It is to be known that change is natural and does not mean there need be fear.

It is the Mother Earth shifting in her chair and taking a different view of her surroundings.

That's a lovely way of describing it.

You've said that you wish to distribute a message to humanity about our environmental situation. We will continue this conversation in depth, yet first: why are we having this conversation about healing Planet Earth *now*?

You are a young civilization on that planet, and whether you survive to be an older and wiser peoples depends now on the speed at which repair to Earth's resources is undertaken and affected. Damage is severe now to your environment, and that combined with greed and diminished integrity of corporate entities and world governments doesn't bode well for healing before a Failsafe point is reached.

If we weren't to change anything and continued on this current destruction trajectory, is the Failsafe point rather soon—in my lifetime? Some say that the Earth only has eight or maybe twelve years left before we've reached the tipping point of "too late"—that Failsafe point, as you say. Would eight to twelve years be considered about right? I know that you don't speak in linear time, yet please pin this down to an estimated timeline as this will help when communicating this message.

Yes, it is the case that in the very soon time is the Failsafe point we referred to. It is here that a line is drawn in the sand and if minds and hearts aren't changed to the extent that actions are changed, your Planet Earth will continue down the path to the point of no return. This is serious and non-reversible. It is to be respected.

• •● ∞ ●• •

About the Author and Channeler

*P*enelope Jean Hayes is a new consciousness author, television personality, and speaker. She has appeared on-camera hundreds of times as an expert guest on programs including *Dr. Phil*, *ABC News*, as well as international news specials and telecasts. She is the foremost leader in the field of contagious and osmotic energy known as Viralenology, founder of the Viral Energy Institute, and author of the book *The Magic of Viral Energy: An Ancient Key to Happiness, Empowerment, and Purpose*.

Carole Serene Borgens channels Pax, the Divine Wisdom Source. Carole is a former nurse and longtime student of metaphysics. She has been channeling Spirit since the early 1990s when she was chosen by Pax and given the title "Spirit Messenger". Carole continues to write and provide in-person and remote sessions for clients around the globe, and she refers to her gift of channeling as "the greatest blessing in my life."

Of this trio, Pax says, "A good team we three."

www.PaxWisdom.com
www.PenelopeJeanHayes.com
www.CaroleSereneBorgens.com

www.ingramcontent.com/pod-product-compliance
Lightning Source LLC
Chambersburg PA
CBHW031521040426
42445CB00009B/336